The Women's Wellbeing
Journal

The Women's Wellbeing

Journal

This Journal belongs to:

....

The Women's Wellbeing

Journal

Phenomenal Woman
Maya Angelou

Pretty women wonder where my secret lies.
I'm not cute or built to suit a fashion model's size
But when I start to tell them,
They think I'm telling lies.
I say,
It's in the reach of my arms
The span of my hips,
The stride of my step,
The curl of my lips.
I'm a woman
Phenomenally.
Phenomenal woman,
That's me.

Introduction:

Getting your thoughts down on paper is a great self-care exercise.

With daily prompts, this journal will help you to get the thoughts from your head on to the paper.

Remember - your journal is private, it is your own space. Unless YOU decide otherwise, your eyes will be the only ones that will see it.

So, be yourself, be authentic, be honest and perhaps after 120 days of journaling you will be surprised what you will have learned about yourself.

It's going to be a great adventure - enjoy!

How to use this journal:

In addition to the 120 daily pages, this journal also offers you some support material:

- Morning routine - embrace the day!

- Evening routine - prepare for a good night's sleep.

- Intentions - set them in a variety of areas.

- A guide to the week ahead.

- A positive quote to end the week.

- A weekly review to see how you are doing.

- Space for additional notes.

How to use this journal:

As with all new habits, the most important thing about journaling is consistency, so to set the routine in motion, try doing the following:

1. Pick a time that works best for you.

2. Use the daily prompt to get you started.

3. Don't overthink it, just get it down on paper.

4. Don't worry if you veer off topic.

5. It will still be YOUR thoughts on the paper.

How to use this journal:

However,

The single most important
instruction is:

ENJOY!

Morning Routine

Wake up:

Try not to snooze, get some natural light on your face, and turn on as many lights as you can to signal to your body that it's time to be awake. If you don't shower immediately, try washing your face right after getting up to help your eyes feel more awake, too.

Overcome sleep inertia:

Move your body, listen to some upbeat music, and talk to another human if you can. These activities can help you throw off the sluggish feeling of sleep more quickly, and stop you from wanting to go back to bed once you're up.

Start your day well:

Make time to work towards your goals, work on personal projects, clear your mind, and spend time with people you care about. Start your day in a way that matches your values and puts you in a great mood.

Evening Routine

Bedtime:

Having a set bedtime can enable your brain to begin the slow-down process before you head to the bedroom. We are creatures of habit and establishing a time for bed and not just a regular alarm call in the morning can help with sleep patterns.

Ditch the Technology:

Try turning off all your electronic devices an hour before bedtime, this helps stop stimulating your brain and again tells your brain that it's time for bed!

End your day well:

A little self-care can promote a good night's sleep. Consider doing a short meditation before bed, taking a warm bath or relaxing with a good book.

My Intentions

Family

Exercise

Nutrition

Self-Care

New Habit

Relaxation

The Week Ahead:

This week's affirmation:

I am confident and value myself.

This week's challenge:

Call someone you love but have not spoken to for a while.

Daily prompt: *What have you done lately just for you?*

....
....
....
....
....
....
....
....
....
....
....
....
....

"

Today I am grateful for:

"

*My thoughts –
positive or negative:*

"

*Today I will practice self-
compassion by.....*

Tomorrow is going to be a great day because:

Daily prompt: *What is your favorite memory?*

....
....
....
....
....
....
....
....
....
....
....
....
....
....

"

Today I am grateful for:

"

My thoughts –
positive or negative:

"

Today I will practice self-
compassion by.....

Tomorrow is going to be a great day because:

Daily prompt: *What are you most grateful for right now?*

....
....
....
....
....
....
....
....
....
....
....
....
....

❝

Today I am grateful for:

❞

❝

*My thoughts –
positive or negative:*

❞

❝

*Today I will practice self-
compassion by.....*

❞

Tomorrow is going to be a great day because:

Daily prompt: *What thought patterns are holding you back right now?*

"

Today I am grateful for:

"

"

*My thoughts –
positive or negative:*

"

"

*Today I will practice self-
compassion by.....*

"

Tomorrow is going to be a great day because:

Daily prompt: *What are you afraid of?*

....
....
....
....
....
....
....
....
....
....
....
....
....

66

Today I am grateful for:

99

66

*My thoughts –
positive or negative:*

99

66

*Today I will practice self-
compassion by.....*

99

Tomorrow is going to be a great day because:

Daily prompt: *What does success mean to you?*

Today I am grateful for:

My thoughts -
positive or negative:

Today I will practice self-
compassion by.....

Tomorrow is going to be a great day because:

Daily prompt: *What limiting beliefs are holding you back from living your dream life?*

....
....
....
....
....
....
....
....
....
....
....
....
....
....

"

Today I am grateful for:

"

My thoughts – positive or negative:

"

Today I will practice self-compassion by.....

Tomorrow is going to be a great day because:

A Positive Quote
to end the week:

"*Courage starts with showing up and letting ourselves be seen.*"

Brene Brown

Small wins this week:

1.

2.

3.

Areas I need to focus on next week:

1.

2.

3.

I am proud that:

I am excited that:

I am surprised by:

Additional thoughts:

The Week Ahead:

This week's affirmation:

I am growing and learning every day.

This week's challenge:

Meditate each day for 5 minutes.

Daily prompt: *What are you grateful for this week?*

....
....
....
....
....
....
....
....
....
....
....
....
....
....
....

"

Today I am grateful for:

"

My thoughts –
positive or negative:

"

Today I will practice self-
compassion by.....

Tomorrow is going to be a great day because:

Daily prompt: *What have you done lately that you are proud of?*

....
....
....
....
....
....
....
....
....
....
....
....
....
....
....

"
Today I am grateful for:

"
My thoughts –
positive or negative:

"
Today I will practice self-compassion by.....

Tomorrow is going to be a great day because:

Daily prompt: *What are your priorities for this year?*

....
....
....
....
....
....
....
....
....
....
....
....
....
....

66

Today I am grateful for:

66

*My thoughts –
positive or negative:*

66

*Today I will practice self-
compassion by.....*

99   **99**   **99**

Tomorrow is going to be a great day because:

Daily prompt: *What is one adjustment you would like to make to your morning routine?*

....
....
....
....
....
....
....
....
....
....
....
....
....
....

"
Today I am grateful for:

"
My thoughts –
positive or negative:

"
Today I will practice self-
compassion by.....

Tomorrow is going to be a great day because:

Daily prompt: *What is one adjustment you would like to make to your evening routine?*

....
....
....
....
....
....
....
....
....
....
....
....
....
....

"

Today I am grateful for:

"

My thoughts –
positive or negative:

"

Today I will practice self-
compassion by.....

Tomorrow is going to be a great day because:

Daily prompt: *How do you remind yourself that you are enough?*

_____

_____

_____

_____

_____

_____

_____

_____

_____

_____

_____

_____

_____

"

Today I am grateful for:

"

"

My thoughts –
positive or negative:

"

"

Today I will practice self-
compassion by.....

"

Tomorrow is going to be a great day because:

Daily prompt: *What is your ultimate goal in life?*

....
....
....
....
....
....
....
....
....
....
....
....
....
....
....

"

Today I am grateful for:

"

*My thoughts –
positive or negative:*

"

*Today I will practice self-
compassion by.....*

Tomorrow is going to be a great day because:

A Positive Quote to end the week:

"*The perfect moment is this one.*"

Jon Kabat Zinn

Weekly Review

Small wins this week:

1.

2.

3.

Areas I need to focus on next week:

1.

2.

3.

I am proud that:

I am excited that:

I am surprised by:

Additional thoughts:

The Week Ahead:

This week's affirmation:

I believe in myself and my skills.

This week's challenge:

Do something you have been putting off for a while.

Daily prompt: *What is causing you stress right now?*

....
....
....
....
....
....
....
....
....
....
....
....
....
....

"

Today I am grateful for:

"

*My thoughts –
positive or negative:*

"

Today I will practice self-compassion by.....

Tomorrow is going to be a great day because:

Daily prompt: *What is one thing you can do today to reduce stress in your life?*

....

....

....

....

....

....

....

....

....

....

....

....

....

....

66

Today I am grateful for:

99

66

My thoughts –
positive or negative:

99

66

Today I will practice self-compassion by.....

99

Tomorrow is going to be a great day because:

Daily prompt: *If I could talk to my younger self, the one thing I would say is....*

....
....
....
....
....
....
....
....
....
....
....
....
....

Today I am grateful for:

My thoughts – positive or negative:

Today I will practice self-compassion by.....

Tomorrow is going to be a great day because:

Daily prompt: *Describe the most unforgettable moment in your life.*

....
....
....
....
....
....
....
....
....
....
....
....
....
....

"

Today I am grateful for:

"

My thoughts –
positive or negative:

"

Today I will practice self-
compassion by.....

Tomorrow is going to be a great day because:

Daily prompt: *Name what is enough for you.*

....
....
....
....
....
....
....
....
....
....
....
....
....
....

66

Today I am grateful for:

99

66

*My thoughts –
positive or negative:*

99

66

*Today I will practice self-
compassion by.....*

99

Tomorrow is going to be a great day because:

Daily prompt: *What do you love about life?*

....

....

....

....

....

....

....

....

....

....

....

....

....

....

....

....

"

Today I am grateful for:

"

My thoughts – positive or negative:

"

Today I will practice self-compassion by.....

Tomorrow is going to be a great day because:

Daily prompt: *Describe yourself in 10 words or less.*

66

Today I am grateful for:

99

66

*My thoughts –
positive or negative:*

99

66

*Today I will practice self-
compassion by.....*

99

Tomorrow is going to be a great day because:

A Positive Quote
to end the week:

"*I am the greatest. I said that even before I knew I was.*"

Muhammad Ali

Small wins this week:

1.

2.

3.

Areas I need to focus on next week:

1.

2.

3.

I am proud that:

I am excited that:

I am surprised by:

Additional thoughts:

The Week Ahead:

This week's affirmation:

I have the power to change the world.

This week's challenge:

Don't compare yourself to others this week.

Daily prompt: *Write about a failure you had. What can you learn from that?*

....
....
....
....
....
....
....
....
....
....
....
....
....
....

"

Today I am grateful for:

"

*My thoughts –
positive or negative:*

"

Today I will practice self-compassion by.....

Tomorrow is going to be a great day because:

Daily prompt: *Make a list of everything you would like to say 'no' to. How many of these are you currently doing?*

Today I am grateful for:

My thoughts –
positive or negative:

Today I will practice self-compassion by.....

Tomorrow is going to be a great day because:

Daily prompt: *Make a list of everything you would like to say 'yes' to. How many of these are you currently doing?*

....
....
....
....
....
....
....
....
....
....
....
....
....
....

66

Today I am grateful for:

99

66

*My thoughts –
positive or negative:*

99

66

Today I will practice self-compassion by.....

99

Tomorrow is going to be a great day because:

Daily prompt: *How will making myself a priority positively impact my life?*

....
....
....
....
....
....
....
....
....
....
....
....
....
....

66

Today I am grateful for:

99

66

My thoughts – positive or negative:

99

66

Today I will practice self-compassion by.....

99

Tomorrow is going to be a great day because:

Daily prompt: *What are 3 things that I am currently doing that no longer serve me? How can I stop doing these things?*

....
....
....
....
....
....
....
....
....
....
....
....
....
....

"

Today I am grateful for:

"

*My thoughts –
positive or negative:*

"

*Today I will practice self-
compassion by.....*

Tomorrow is going to be a great day because:

Daily prompt: *What can I do to add more flow and relaxation to my day?*

> **"**
>
> *Today I am grateful for:*
>
> **"**

> **"**
>
> *My thoughts –*
> *positive or negative:*
>
> **"**

> **"**
>
> *Today I will practice self-compassion by.....*
>
> **"**

Tomorrow is going to be a great day because:

Daily prompt: *When I am really busy, how can I find 10 minutes of time for myself? What can I do in that time?*

....
....
....
....
....
....
....
....
....
....
....
....
....
....
....

"

Today I am grateful for:

"

"

*My thoughts –
positive or negative:*

"

"

Today I will practice self-compassion by.....

"

Tomorrow is going to be a great day because:

A Positive Quote to end the week:

"I've learned that people will forget what you said, people will forget what you did, but people will never forget how you made them feel."

Maya Angelou

Weekly Review

Small wins this week:

1.

2.

3.

Areas I need to focus on next week:

1.

2.

3.

I am proud that:

I am excited that:

I am surprised by:

Additional thoughts:

_____

_____

_____

_____

The Week Ahead:

This week's affirmation:

I can do anything I set my mind to.

This week's challenge:

Don't complain about things this week.

Daily prompt: *Write a letter of gratitude to yourself for looking after your own wellbeing.*

....

....

....

....

....

....

....

....

....

....

....

....

....

....

"

Today I am grateful for:

"

"

*My thoughts –
positive or negative:*

"

"

Today I will practice self-compassion by.....

"

Tomorrow is going to be a great day because:

Daily prompt: *What is one positive habit I can make in my daily life?*

....
....
....
....
....
....
....
....
....
....
....
....
....
....

"

Today I am grateful for:

"

*My thoughts –
positive or negative:*

"

*Today I will practice self-
compassion by.....*

Tomorrow is going to be a great day because:

Daily prompt: *Consider your mindset. Is it serving you? How can you make a shift if it isn't working for you?*

....
....
....
....
....
....
....
....
....
....
....
....
....
....

"

Today I am grateful for:

"

*My thoughts –
positive or negative:*

"

*Today I will practice self-
compassion by.....*

Tomorrow is going to be a great day because:

Daily prompt: *How can you celebrate yourself today?*

....
....
....
....
....
....
....
....
....
....
....
....
....
....

"

Today I am grateful for:

"

"

*My thoughts –
positive or negative:*

"

"

*Today I will practice self-
compassion by.....*

"

Tomorrow is going to be a great day because:

Daily prompt: *What helps you slow down and feel more present?*

....
....
....
....
....
....
....
....
....
....
....
....
....

"

Today I am grateful for:

"

"

*My thoughts –
positive or negative:*

"

"

Today I will practice self-compassion by.....

"

Tomorrow is going to be a great day because:

Daily prompt: *How do you stay focused and steer clear of distractions?*

....
....
....
....
....
....
....
....
....
....
....
....
....
....
....

"

Today I am grateful for:

"

"

My thoughts –
positive or negative:

"

"

Today I will practice self-
compassion by.....

"

Tomorrow is going to be a great day because:

Daily prompt: *How do you notice when you are nearing burnout?*

....
....
....
....
....
....
....
....
....
....
....
....
....

"

Today I am grateful for:

"

"

*My thoughts –
positive or negative:*

"

"

Today I will practice self-compassion by.....

"

Tomorrow is going to be a great day because:

A Positive Quote
to end the week:

"*You've always had the power my dear, you just had to learn it for yourself.*"

Glinda – The Wizard of Oz

Weekly Review

Small wins this week:

1.

2.

3.

Areas I need to focus on next week:

1.

2.

3.

I am proud that:

I am excited that:

I am surprised by:

Additional thoughts:

_____

_____

_____

_____

The Week Ahead:

This week's affirmation:

I am confident in my abilities.

This week's challenge:

Don't talk badly about another person this week.

Daily prompt: *How do you ask for help or support when you need it?*

....
....
....
....
....
....
....
....
....
....
....
....
....
....

"

Today I am grateful for:

"

"

My thoughts –
positive or negative:

"

"

Today I will practice self-
compassion by.....

"

Tomorrow is going to be a great day because:

Daily prompt: *What things make you happy?*

_____
_____
_____
_____
_____
_____
_____
_____
_____
_____
_____
_____
_____
_____

"

Today I am grateful for:

"

*My thoughts –
positive or negative:*

"

*Today I will practice self-
compassion by.....*

Tomorrow is going to be a great day because:

Daily prompt: *What's a funny story that makes you laugh every time?*

....
....
....
....
....
....
....
....
....
....
....
....
....
....

"

Today I am grateful for:

"

My thoughts –
positive or negative:

"

Today I will practice self-compassion by.....

Tomorrow is going to be a great day because:

Daily prompt: *What brings you genuine joy?*

> **Today I am grateful for:**

> **My thoughts –**
> *positive or negative:*

> **Today I will practice self-compassion by.....**

Tomorrow is going to be a great day because:

Daily prompt: *What makes you happiest in life?*

....
....
....
....
....
....
....
....
....
....
....
....
....
....

"

Today I am grateful for:

"

*My thoughts –
positive or negative:*

"

*Today I will practice self-
compassion by.....*

Tomorrow is going to be a great day because:

Daily prompt: *What are you proud of yourself for?*

....
....
....
....
....
....
....
....
....
....
....
....
....

"

Today I am grateful for:

"

*My thoughts –
positive or negative:*

"

*Today I will practice self-
compassion by.....*

Tomorrow is going to be a great day because:

Daily prompt: *One thing I need to work on is....*

....

....

....

....

....

....

....

....

....

....

....

....

"

Today I am grateful for:

"

*My thoughts –
positive or negative:*

"

*Today I will practice self-
compassion by.....*

,,

,,

,,

Tomorrow is going to be a great day because:

*A Positive Quote
to end the week:*

"*Be thankful for what you
have; you'll end up having
more. If you concentrate on
what you don't have, you will
never, ever have enough.*"

Oprah Winfrey

Weekly Review

Small wins this week:

1.

2.

3.

Areas I need to focus on next week:

1.

2.

3.

I am proud that:

I am excited that:

I am surprised by:

Additional thoughts:

The Week Ahead:

This week's affirmation:

I grow with every challenge.

This week's challenge:

Take a break from social media this week.

Daily prompt: *What do you need to forgive yourself for?*

....
....
....
....
....
....
....
....
....
....
....
....
....
....
....

"

Today I am grateful for:

"

"

*My thoughts –
positive or negative:*

"

"

*Today I will practice self-
compassion by.....*

"

Tomorrow is going to be a great day because:

Daily prompt: *Name a habit you need to stop doing to live a more meaningful life?*

_____

_____

_____

_____

_____

_____

_____

_____

_____

_____

_____

_____

_____

_____

"

Today I am grateful for:

"

*My thoughts –
positive or negative:*

"

Today I will practice self-compassion by.....

Tomorrow is going to be a great day because:

Daily prompt: *What is your proudest moment?*

....
....
....
....
....
....
....
....
....
....
....
....
....
....

66

Today I am grateful for:

66

My thoughts –
positive or negative:

66

Today I will practice self-
compassion by.....

Tomorrow is going to be a great day because:

Daily prompt: *What makes you feel powerful?*

---

66 Today I am grateful for:

66 My thoughts –
positive or negative:

66 Today I will practice self-compassion by.....

Tomorrow is going to be a great day because:

Daily prompt: *What could you do to make your life more joyful every day?*

....
....
....
....
....
....
....
....
....
....
....
....
....
....

"

Today I am grateful for:

"

"

*My thoughts –
positive or negative:*

"

"

Today I will practice self-compassion by.....

"

Tomorrow is going to be a great day because:

Daily prompt: *How can I show myself more love?*

....
....
....
....
....
....
....
....
....
....
....
....
....
....

"

Today I am grateful for:

"

"

*My thoughts -
positive or negative:*

"

"

Today I will practice self-compassion by.....

"

Tomorrow is going to be a great day because:

Daily prompt: *When do you feel most confident?*

_____

_____

_____

_____

_____

_____

_____

_____

_____

_____

_____

_____

_____

_____

"

Today I am grateful for:

"

"

My thoughts –
positive or negative:

"

"

Today I will practice self-
compassion by.....

"

Tomorrow is going to be a great day because:

A Positive Quote
to end the week:

"It is impossible to live
without failing at something,
unless you live so cautiously
that you might as well not
have lived at all – in which
case, you fail by default."

J. K. Rowling

Weekly Review

Small wins this week:

1.

2.

3.

Areas I need to focus on next week:

1.

2.

3.

I am proud that:

I am excited that:

I am surprised by:

Additional thoughts:

The Week Ahead:

This week's affirmation:

I am consistent in my hard work.

This week's challenge:

Practice saying 'no' to things you don't want, or need, to do.

Daily prompt: *Make a list of 30 things that make you smile.*

> ❝
>
> *Today I am grateful for:*
>
> ❞

> ❝
>
> *My thoughts –*
> *positive or negative:*
>
> ❞

> ❝
>
> *Today I will practice self-compassion by.....*
>
> ❞

Tomorrow is going to be a great day because:

Daily prompt: *What does unconditional love look like for you?*

....

....

....

....

....

....

....

....

....

....

....

....

....

....

"
Today I am grateful for:

"

"
*My thoughts –
positive or negative:*

"

"
*Today I will practice self-
compassion by.....*

"

Tomorrow is going to be a great day because:

Daily prompt: *Write the words that would make you happier today.*

....
....
....
....
....
....
....
....
....
....
....
....
....
....

"

Today I am grateful for:

"

"

*My thoughts –
positive or negative:*

"

"

*Today I will practice self-
compassion by.....*

"

Tomorrow is going to be a great day because:

Daily prompt: *What acts of self-care truly make me happy? How can I add more of this to my self-care routine?*

"

Today I am grateful for:

"

"

My thoughts –
positive or negative:

"

"

Today I will practice self-compassion by.....

"

Tomorrow is going to be a great day because:

Daily prompt: *I feel happiest when....*

_____

_____

_____

_____

_____

_____

_____

_____

_____

_____

_____

_____

_____

"

Today I am grateful for:

"

"

*My thoughts –
positive or negative:*

"

"

*Today I will practice self-
compassion by.....*

"

Tomorrow is going to be a great day because:

Daily prompt: *What personal needs am I sacrificing to meet the needs of others?*

....
....
....
....
....
....
....
....
....
....
....
....
....

"

Today I am grateful for:

"

*My thoughts –
positive or negative:*

"

Today I will practice self-compassion by.....

Tomorrow is going to be a great day because:

Daily prompt: *What makes me feel calm?*

"

Today I am grateful for:

"

"

My thoughts -
positive or negative:

"

"

Today I will practice self-compassion by.....

"

Tomorrow is going to be a great day because:

*A Positive Quote
to end the week:*

"*Be who you are and say what
you feel because those who
mind don't matter and those
who matter don't mind.*"

Dr. Seuss

Small wins this week:

1.

2.

3.

Areas I need to focus on next week:

1.

2.

3.

I am proud that:

I am excited that:

I am surprised by:

Additional thoughts:

The Week Ahead:

This week's affirmation:

*I have or can easily get everything
I need to succeed.*

This week's challenge:

Practice setting boundaries.

Daily prompt: *What makes you feel in control?*

"

Today I am grateful for:

"

*My thoughts –
positive or negative:*

"

*Today I will practice self-
compassion by.....*

Tomorrow is going to be a great day because:

Daily prompt: *How do you put yourself first without feeling guilty?*

....
....
....
....
....
....
....
....
....
....
....
....
....
....

"

Today I am grateful for:

"

"

*My thoughts –
positive or negative:*

"

"

*Today I will practice self-
compassion by.....*

"

Tomorrow is going to be a great day because:

Daily prompt: *How do you practice self-acceptance?*

....
....
....
....
....
....
....
....
....
....
....
....
....
....

"

Today I am grateful for:

"

*My thoughts -
positive or negative:*

"

*Today I will practice self-
compassion by.....*

Tomorrow is going to be a great day because:

Daily prompt: *How do you set boundaries and avoid taking on someone else's emotions and stress?*

....
....
....
....
....
....
....
....
....
....
....
....
....
....

"

Today I am grateful for:

"

"

*My thoughts –
positive or negative:*

"

"

*Today I will practice self-
compassion by.....*

"

Tomorrow is going to be a great day because:

Daily prompt: *How do you advocate for yourself?*

_____
_____
_____
_____
_____
_____
_____
_____
_____
_____
_____
_____
_____
_____

> **"**
> *Today I am grateful for:*
>
> **"**

> **"**
> *My thoughts –*
> *positive or negative:*
>
> **"**

> **"**
> *Today I will practice self-compassion by.....*
>
> **"**

Tomorrow is going to be a great day because:

Daily prompt: *How do you forgive yourself when you make a mistake?*

....
....
....
....
....
....
....
....
....
....
....
....
....
....

"

Today I am grateful for:

"

"

My thoughts – positive or negative:

"

"

Today I will practice self-compassion by.....

"

Tomorrow is going to be a great day because:

Daily prompt: *How do you calm your nerves in a difficult situation?*

....

....

....

....

....

....

....

....

....

....

....

....

....

....

"

Today I am grateful for:

"

My thoughts - positive or negative:

"

Today I will practice self-compassion by.....

"

Tomorrow is going to be a great day because:

*A Positive Quote
to end the week:*

"*Success is getting what you
want. Happiness is wanting
what you get.*"

Dale Carnegie

Weekly Review

Small wins this week:

1.

2.

3.

Areas I need to focus on next week:

1.

2.

3.

I am proud that:

I am excited that:

I am surprised by:

Additional thoughts:

_____

_____

_____

_____

The Week Ahead:

This week's affirmation:

I let go of limiting beliefs and choose to trust myself.

This week's challenge:

Take a break from alcohol for 28 days.

Daily prompt: *How do you trust yourself to make big decisions?*

....
....
....
....
....
....
....
....
....
....
....
....
....
....

"

Today I am grateful for:

"

*My thoughts –
positive or negative:*

"

*Today I will practice self-
compassion by.....*

Tomorrow is going to be a great day because:

Daily prompt: *What does your dream life look like?*

"

Today I am grateful for:

"

My thoughts –
positive or negative:

"

Today I will practice self-
compassion by.....

Tomorrow is going to be a great day because:

Daily prompt: *What do you want your life to look like 3 years from now?*

....

....

....

....

....

....

....

....

....

....

....

....

....

....

....

"

Today I am grateful for:

"

My thoughts -
positive or negative:

"

Today I will practice self-
compassion by.....

Tomorrow is going to be a great day because:

Daily prompt: *What do you want your legacy to be?*

....

....

....

....

....

....

....

....

....

....

....

....

....

"

Today I am grateful for:

"

"

*My thoughts –
positive or negative:*

"

"

*Today I will practice self-
compassion by.....*

"

Tomorrow is going to be a great day because:

Daily prompt: *What do you need to let go of?*

....

....

....

....

....

....

....

....

....

....

....

....

....

....

"

Today I am grateful for:

"

"

My thoughts -
positive or negative:

"

"

Today I will practice self-
compassion by.....

"

Tomorrow is going to be a great day because:

Daily prompt: *What would your ideal day look like?*

....
....
....
....
....
....
....
....
....
....
....
....
....
....

"
Today I am grateful for:

"
*My thoughts –
positive or negative:*

"
*Today I will practice self-
compassion by.....*

Tomorrow is going to be a great day because:

Daily prompt: *What do you need most to heal right now?*

....
....
....
....
....
....
....
....
....
....
....
....
....
....

"

Today I am grateful for:

"

*My thoughts –
positive or negative:*

"

*Today I will practice self-
compassion by.....*

Tomorrow is going to be a great day because:

*A Positive Quote
to end the week:*

"*Have no fear of perfection;
you'll never reach it.*"

Marie Curie

Weekly Review

Small wins this week:

1.

2.

3.

Areas I need to focus on next week:

1.

2.

3.

I am proud that:

I am excited that:

I am surprised by:

Additional thoughts:

The Week Ahead:

This week's affirmation:

My power is unlimited.

This week's challenge:

Replace 'you should's with 'you could's.

Daily prompt: *What do you need to forgive yourself for?*

....
....
....
....
....
....
....
....
....
....
....
....
....

"

Today I am grateful for:

"

"

*My thoughts –
positive or negative:*

"

"

*Today I will practice self-
compassion by.....*

"

Tomorrow is going to be a great day because:

Daily prompt: *What would you do if it was impossible to fail?*

....
....
....
....
....
....
....
....
....
....
....
....
....

❝

Today I am grateful for:

❞

❝

*My thoughts –
positive or negative:*

❞

❝

*Today I will practice self-
compassion by.....*

❞

Tomorrow is going to be a great day because:

Daily prompt: *What do you wish you had more time for?*

....
....
....
....
....
....
....
....
....
....
....
....
....
....

"

Today I am grateful for:

"

"

My thoughts –
positive or negative:

"

"

Today I will practice self-
compassion by.....

"

Tomorrow is going to be a great day because:

Daily prompt: *What's the best dream you can remember?*

....
....
....
....
....
....
....
....
....
....
....
....
....
....

"
Today I am grateful for:

"
My thoughts –
positive or negative:

"
Today I will practice self-
compassion by.....

Tomorrow is going to be a great day because:

Daily prompt: *A mantra I would like to live by is....*

66

Today I am grateful for:

99

66

My thoughts –
positive or negative:

99

66

Today I will practice self-
compassion by.....

99

Tomorrow is going to be a great day because:

Daily prompt: *What would you do if you loved yourself unconditionally?*
How would you treat yourself and how can you start doing that now?

....
....
....
....
....
....
....
....
....
....
....
....
....
....

❝

Today I am grateful for:

❝

My thoughts –
positive or negative:

❝

Today I will practice self-
compassion by.....

Tomorrow is going to be a great day because:

Daily prompt: *Is my morning serving me well? What does it look like? Do I have a routine? Are mornings rushed?*

....

....

....

....

....

....

....

....

....

....

....

....

....

....

"
Today I am grateful for:

"
My thoughts – positive or negative:

"
Today I will practice self-compassion by.....

Tomorrow is going to be a great day because:

A Positive Quote
to end the week:

"*If you're always trying to be normal, you will never know how amazing you can be.*"

Maya Angelou

Small wins this week:

1.

2.

3.

Areas I need to focus on next week:

1.

2.

3.

I am proud that:

I am excited that:

I am surprised by:

Additional thoughts:

_____

_____

_____

_____

The Week Ahead:

This week's affirmation:

I know I can face every challenge with ease, there is nothing I cannot overcome.

This week's challenge:

Practice Yoga.

Daily prompt: *I am the best version of myself when I....*

....

....

....

....

....

....

....

....

....

....

....

....

....

....

....

"

Today I am grateful for:

"

*My thoughts –
positive or negative:*

"

*Today I will practice self-
compassion by.....*

Tomorrow is going to be a great day because:

Daily prompt: *Am I living in alignment with my values? What can I change to make this happen?*

....
....
....
....
....
....
....
....
....
....
....
....
....

"

Today I am grateful for:

"

*My thoughts –
positive or negative:*

"

*Today I will practice self-
compassion by.....*

Tomorrow is going to be a great day because:

Daily prompt: *How do you savor the time you get alone?*

....

....

....

....

....

....

....

....

....

....

....

....

....

"

Today I am grateful for:

"

My thoughts –
positive or negative:

"

Today I will practice self-
compassion by.....

Tomorrow is going to be a great day because:

Daily prompt: *How do you embrace your true self, even if it looks different from what others expect?*

"
Today I am grateful for:

"
My thoughts – positive or negative:

"
Today I will practice self-compassion by.....

Tomorrow is going to be a great day because:

Daily prompt: *Write a letter to yourself from the future version of you. Tell yourself how awesome your life is now.*

....

....

....

....

....

....

....

....

....

....

....

....

....

"

Today I am grateful for:

"

"

*My thoughts -
positive or negative:*

"

"

Today I will practice self-compassion by.....

"

Tomorrow is going to be a great day because:

Daily prompt: *If you could make a living doing anything, what would it be?*

....
....
....
....
....
....
....
....
....
....
....
....
....
....

> 66

Today I am grateful for:

> 66

My thoughts – positive or negative:

> 66

Today I will practice self-compassion by.....

Tomorrow is going to be a great day because:

Daily prompt: *What are some things that inspire you?*

....

....

....

....

....

....

....

....

....

....

....

....

....

....

"

Today I am grateful for:

"

*My thoughts -
positive or negative:*

"

*Today I will practice self-
compassion by.....*

Tomorrow is going to be a great day because:

A Positive Quote
to end the week:

"*Real change, enduring change, happens one step at a time.*"

Ruth Bader Ginsburg

Weekly Review

Small wins this week:

1.

2.

3.

Areas I need to focus on next week:

1.

2.

3.

I am proud that:

I am excited that:

I am surprised by:

Additional thoughts:

_____

_____

_____

The Week Ahead:

This week's affirmation:

I am creating my dream life every single day.

This week's challenge:

Practice breathing techniques.

Daily prompt: *If I could accomplish one thing in the next 3 months, what would it be?*

....
....
....
....
....
....
....
....
....
....
....
....
....
....

"

Today I am grateful for:

"

My thoughts – positive or negative:

"

Today I will practice self-compassion by.....

Tomorrow is going to be a great day because:

Daily prompt: *A topic you want to learn about that will help you be happier? How can you start learning about it?*

....
....
....
....
....
....
....
....
....
....
....
....
....
....

"
Today I am grateful for:

"
My thoughts –
positive or negative:

"
Today I will practice self-compassion by.....

Tomorrow is going to be a great day because:

Daily prompt: *How can I encourage myself when I'm trying something new?*

....
....
....
....
....
....
....
....
....
....
....
....
....
....

"

Today I am grateful for:

"

"

*My thoughts –
positive or negative:*

"

"

Today I will practice self-compassion by.....

"

Tomorrow is going to be a great day because:

Daily prompt: *What can you do today that you didn't think you could do a year ago?*

....
....
....
....
....
....
....
....
....
....
....
....
....
....

"

Today I am grateful for:

"

My thoughts – positive or negative:

"

Today I will practice self-compassion by.....

Tomorrow is going to be a great day because:

Daily prompt: *How can you step outside your comfort zone to grow?*

....

....

....

....

....

....

....

....

....

....

....

....

....

....

"

Today I am grateful for:

"

My thoughts –
positive or negative:

"

Today I will practice self-
compassion by.....

Tomorrow is going to be a great day because:

Daily prompt: *If you could take a vacation anywhere in the world, where would it be?*

....
....
....
....
....
....
....
....
....
....
....
....
....
....

> ❝
> Today I am grateful for:
> ❞

> ❝
> My thoughts –
> positive or negative:
> ❞

> ❝
> Today I will practice self-
> compassion by.....
> ❞

Tomorrow is going to be a great day because:

Daily prompt: *What do I need more of in my life?*

....
....
....
....
....
....
....
....
....
....
....
....
....

"
Today I am grateful for:

"

"
My thoughts –
positive or negative:

"

"
Today I will practice self-
compassion by.....

"

Tomorrow is going to be a great day because:

A Positive Quote to end the week:

"*The most difficult thing is the decision to act. The rest is merely tenacity.*"

Amelia Earhart

Small wins this week:

1.

2.

3.

Areas I need to focus on next week:

1.

2.

3.

I am proud that:

I am excited that:

I am surprised by:

Additional thoughts:

The Week Ahead:

This week's affirmation:

I show up every day and do my best.

This week's challenge:

Try something new this week.

Daily prompt: *When you wake up in the morning, how do you want to feel?*

....
....
....
....
....
....
....
....
....
....
....
....
....

66

Today I am grateful for:

99

66

My thoughts – positive or negative:

99

66

Today I will practice self-compassion by.....

99

Tomorrow is going to be a great day because:

Daily prompt: *How do you add value to the world?*

....
....
....
....
....
....
....
....
....
....
....
....
....
....

"

Today I am grateful for:

"

My thoughts –
positive or negative:

"

Today I will practice self-
compassion by.....

Tomorrow is going to be a great day because:

Daily prompt: *My favorite way to spend the day is...*

_____
_____
_____
_____
_____
_____
_____
_____
_____
_____
_____
_____
_____

"

Today I am grateful for:

"

My thoughts –
positive or negative:

"

Today I will practice self-
compassion by.....

Tomorrow is going to be a great day because:

Daily prompt: *I couldn't imagine living without...*

....

....

....

....

....

....

....

....

....

....

....

....

....

....

"

Today I am grateful for:

"

My thoughts –
positive or negative:

"

Today I will practice self-
compassion by.....

Tomorrow is going to be a great day because:

Daily prompt: *A space in my home that makes me feel happy is...*

....
....
....
....
....
....
....
....
....
....
....
....
....
....

❝

Today I am grateful for:

❞

❝

*My thoughts –
positive or negative:*

❞

❝

*Today I will practice self-
compassion by.....*

❞

Tomorrow is going to be a great day because:

Daily prompt: *When is the best time in my time to practice self-care?*

....
....
....
....
....
....
....
....
....
....
....
....
....
....
....

"

Today I am grateful for:

"

*My thoughts –
positive or negative:*

"

Today I will practice self-compassion by.....

Tomorrow is going to be a great day because:

Daily prompt: *I am grateful to money because....*

....
....
....
....
....
....
....
....
....
....
....
....
....
....

"

Today I am grateful for:

"

*My thoughts –
positive or negative:*

"

*Today I will practice self-
compassion by.....*

,,　　　**,,**　　　**,,**

Tomorrow is going to be a great day because:

A Positive Quote
to end the week:

"Some people are old at 18 and some are young at 90. Time is a concept that humans created."

Yoko Ono

Weekly Review

Small wins this week:

1.

2.

3.

Areas I need to focus on next week:

1.

2.

3.

I am proud that:

I am excited that:

I am surprised by:

Additional thoughts:

_____

_____

_____

_____

The Week Ahead:

This week's affirmation:

*I believe in my abilities and express
my true self with ease.*

This week's challenge:

Try some new foods this week.

Daily prompt: *Write all of the ways money will help you to live to your fullest potential.*

....
....
....
....
....
....
....
....
....
....
....
....
....
....
....

66

Today I am grateful for:

66

My thoughts – positive or negative:

66

Today I will practice self-compassion by.....

99   **99**   **99**

Tomorrow is going to be a great day because:

Daily prompt: *What feelings come up when I think about my desire for money?*

....
....
....
....
....
....
....
....
....
....
....
....
....
....
....

"

Today I am grateful for:

"

My thoughts - positive or negative:

"

Today I will practice self-compassion by.....

Tomorrow is going to be a great day because:

Daily prompt: *What did your parents teach you about money?*

Today I am grateful for:

My thoughts – positive or negative:

Today I will practice self-compassion by.....

Tomorrow is going to be a great day because:

Daily prompt: *What is my biggest challenge with managing money?*
What step can I take to change that?

....
....
....
....
....
....
....
....
....
....
....
....
....
....

"

Today I am grateful for:

"

My thoughts –
positive or negative:

"

Today I will practice self-
compassion by.....

Tomorrow is going to be a great day because:

Daily prompt: *What is your ideal income? How would your life be impacted as a result of earning this amount?*

....
....
....
....
....
....
....
....
....
....
....
....
....
....

"

Today I am grateful for:

"

*My thoughts –
positive or negative:*

"

Today I will practice self-compassion by.....

Tomorrow is going to be a great day because:

Daily prompt: *Reflect on a past money mistake? How can you forgive yourself for this?*

....

....

....

....

....

....

....

....

....

....

....

....

....

....

"

Today I am grateful for:

"

"

My thoughts - positive or negative:

"

"

Today I will practice self-compassion by.....

"

Tomorrow is going to be a great day because:

Daily prompt: *What's your favorite physical feature?*

....
....
....
....
....
....
....
....
....
....
....
....
....
....

"

Today I am grateful for:

"

*My thoughts –
positive or negative:*

"

*Today I will practice self-
compassion by.....*

Tomorrow is going to be a great day because:

A Positive Quote
to end the week:

"Let us make our future now,
and let us make our dreams
tomorrow's reality."

Malala Yousafzai

Small wins this week:

1.

2.

3.

Areas I need to focus on next week:

1.

2.

3.

I am proud that:

I am excited that:

I am surprised by:

Additional thoughts:

_____

_____

_____

_____

The Week Ahead:

This week's affirmation:

All I need to succeed is within me.

This week's challenge:

Read a new book this week.

Daily prompt: *What items are in your self-care toolkit?*

....
....
....
....
....
....
....
....
....
....
....
....
....

"

Today I am grateful for:

"

My thoughts –
positive or negative:

"

Today I will practice self-
compassion by.....

Tomorrow is going to be a great day because:

Daily prompt: *Today I can honor my body by....*

....

....

....

....

....

....

....

....

....

....

....

....

....

....

....

> **"**
> *Today I am grateful for:*
> **"**

> **"**
> *My thoughts –*
> *positive or negative:*
> **"**

> **"**
> *Today I will practice self-*
> *compassion by.....*
> **"**

Tomorrow is going to be a great day because:

Daily prompt: *If my body could talk, it would say...*

....
....
....
....
....
....
....
....
....
....
....
....
....

"

Today I am grateful for:

"

My thoughts –
positive or negative:

"

Today I will practice self-
compassion by.....

Tomorrow is going to be a great day because:

Daily prompt: *I feel most energized when....*

....
....
....
....
....
....
....
....
....
....
....
....
....
....

"

Today I am grateful for:

"

My thoughts –
positive or negative:

"

Today I will practice self-
compassion by.....

Tomorrow is going to be a great day because:

Daily prompt: *I feel happiest in my skin when....*

....
....
....
....
....
....
....
....
....
....
....
....
....
....

"

Today I am grateful for:

"

*My thoughts –
positive or negative:*

"

*Today I will practice self-
compassion by.....*

Tomorrow is going to be a great day because:

Daily prompt: *Today my self-care mantra is....*

....

....

....

....

....

....

....

....

....

....

....

....

....

"

Today I am grateful for:

"

My thoughts –
positive or negative:

"

Today I will practice self-
compassion by.....

Tomorrow is going to be a great day because:

Daily prompt: *How do I feel about the importance of practicing self-care?*

....
....
....
....
....
....
....
....
....
....
....
....
....
....
....

"

Today I am grateful for:

"

"

My thoughts – positive or negative:

"

"

Today I will practice self-compassion by.....

"

Tomorrow is going to be a great day because:

A Positive Quote
to end the week:

"You can have many great
ideas in your head, but what
makes the difference is the
action. Without action upon
an idea, there will be no
manifestation, no results and
no reward."

Don Miguel Ruiz

Weekly Review

Small wins this week:

1.

2.

3.

Areas I need to focus on next week:

1.

2.

3.

I am proud that:

I am excited that:

I am surprised by:

Additional thoughts:

The Week Ahead:

This week's affirmation:

I am in full control of my life.

This week's challenge:

Go to bed an hour earlier each night this week.

Daily prompt: *Self-care is important to me because I want to feel....*

....
....
....
....
....
....
....
....
....
....
....
....
....

66
Today I am grateful for:

99

66
*My thoughts –
positive or negative:*

99

66
*Today I will practice self-
compassion by.....*

99

Tomorrow is going to be a great day because:

Daily prompt: *What does bedtime look and feel like? Is there anything I can change for a more restful night's sleep?*

....
....
....
....
....
....
....
....
....
....
....
....
....
....

"

Today I am grateful for:

"

*My thoughts –
positive or negative:*

"

Today I will practice self-compassion by.....

Tomorrow is going to be a great day because:

Daily prompt: *What would I say to someone who thinks that self-care is selfish?*

....
....
....
....
....
....
....
....
....
....
....
....
....
....

"

Today I am grateful for:

"

My thoughts - positive or negative:

"

Today I will practice self-compassion by.....

Tomorrow is going to be a great day because:

Daily prompt: *If someone described me, what would they say?*

....
....
....
....
....
....
....
....
....
....
....
....
....
....
....

"
Today I am grateful for:

"
My thoughts –
positive or negative:

"
Today I will practice self-
compassion by.....

Tomorrow is going to be a great day because:

Daily prompt: *What can wait until next week?*

....

....

....

....

....

....

....

....

....

....

....

....

....

....

"

Today I am grateful for:

"

*My thoughts –
positive or negative:*

"

*Today I will practice self-
compassion by.....*

Tomorrow is going to be a great day because:

Daily prompt: *When do I feel most in tune with myself?*

❝

Today I am grateful for:

❞

❝

*My thoughts –
positive or negative:*

❞

❝

*Today I will practice self-
compassion by.....*

❞

Tomorrow is going to be a great day because:

Daily prompt: *What does every part of my body feel in this moment?*

....
....
....
....
....
....
....
....
....
....
....
....
....
....

66

Today I am grateful for:

99

66

*My thoughts –
positive or negative:*

99

66

*Today I will practice self-
compassion by.....*

99

Tomorrow is going to be a great day because:

*A Positive Quote
to end the week:*

"*Happiness leads to success,
not the other way around.*"

Dean Graziosi

Weekly Review

Small wins this week:

1.

2.

3.

Areas I need to focus on next week:

1.

2.

3.

I am proud that:

I am excited that:

I am surprised by:

Additional thoughts:

_____

_____

_____

_____

The Week Ahead:

This week's affirmation:

I release negative self-talk and do not need validations from others.

This week's challenge:

Walk 10,000 steps a day.

Daily prompt: *What are some things that inspire you?*

....

....

....

....

....

....

....

....

....

....

....

....

❝

Today I am grateful for:

❞

❝

*My thoughts –
positive or negative:*

❞

❝

*Today I will practice self-
compassion by.....*

❞

Tomorrow is going to be a great day because:

Take a bow!

Congratulations!

*You have now completed 120
days of journaling!*

Well done - you're amazing!

Notes:

Notes:

Notes:

Notes:

Notes:

Notes:

Notes:

Notes:

Notes:

Notes: